A Little
Book of
UNI-SPIRATION

T0364050

Running Press
Hachette Book Group
1290 Avenue of the Americas, New York, NY 10104
www.runningpress.com
@Running_Press

First Edition: April 2019

Published by Running Press, an imprint of Perseus Books, LLC
a subsidiary of Hachette Book Group, Inc. The Running Press
name and logo is a trademark of the Hachette Book Group.

The Hachette Speakers Bureau provides a wide range of
authors for speaking events. To find out more, go to
www.hachettespeakersbureau.com or call (866) 376-6591.

The publisher is not responsible for websites (or their content)
that are not owned by the publisher.

ISBN: 978-0-7624-9486-6

Believe in Magic...

For more than two thousand years humans have been on the lookout for the ever-elusive creature— the unicorn. Sought out for their beauty, mystery, and nurturing powers, unicorns have been referenced throughout history. Although no man has ever been able to capture one, the power of a unicorn doesn't rely on seeing, it relies on believing in how magical life truly can be.

Perhaps the best way to capture this mythical creature is to look inside yourself and unleash your own inner unicorn! To start you on your journey we've provided your own mini unicorn head—just squeeze the unicorn to remind you how "fabulous" you are. We've also included more uni-spiration in the following pages with 15 unicorn-inspired ways to have a fabulous day. Let your sparkle shine!

Be a unicorn
in a field of horses.

Rain brings rainbows!

Don't forget to make a

≋ SPLASH ≋

in the puddles.

Center yourself

with yoga.

Have an ice cream treat.

Don't forget the sprinkles!

Rock your most colorful ensemble and take center stage!

Keep a
dream board—
*nothing's too big
to achieve.*

Have an impromptu
chore-doing dance party.
*Find the fun in
the everyday.*

.... ◆ ....

Sing your
favorite song
in the shower.
Look out Hollywood,
you're coming!

.... ◆ ....

Add an extra bit of

SPARKLE

to your ensemble

and own it.

Let your hair down

hair down

–you'll have more fun.

*Perform a daily
act of kindness.*

It will bring you joy.

LOOK FOR
MAGIC IN THE
MUNDANE.
Your surroundings might
surprise you.

Throw a
surprise party
for no reason! Birthdays
aren't the only reason to
CELEBRATE.

BE KIND TO YOURSELF!

A self-care day is *always* a good idea.

Listen to a
friend in need.
Actions speak louder
than words.

This book has been bound using
handcraft methods and
Smyth-sewn to ensure durability.

The box, cover, and interior were
illustrated by Robert Venables and
designed by Rachel Peckman.

The text was written by
Chrissy Kopaczewski.